Shame Eraser

You Can Be Forgiven

By Fletcher Law

Isaiah 1:18 New King James Version (NKJV)

18 *"Come now, and let us reason together," says the Lord, "Though your sins are like scarlet, they shall be as white as snow; though they are red like crimson, they shall be as wool."*

Dedication-

This book is dedicated to my father George Hammond Law Jr. He was quick to forgive and led a life of prayer.

Published by RED CLAY BOOKS

ISBN   978-0-359-55351-8

<u>CONTENTS</u>

Chapter 1

Killer Guilt

If you are drawn to this book, perhaps it is because you are wondering if there is forgiveness for you. You never thought you would be so desperate or hurt. You knew other people have committed horrible sins and crimes, but those are other people. Now you are the one suffering grievous pain and guilt.

The guilt you feel might not be from a "sensational" sin. The size of sin does not weaken the effects of sin on one's life. Sin kills our soul and joy. Sin is a disease of the soul that leaves a scar like smallpox does on the skin. This scarring effect on our heart and mind is called shame.

The guilt of murder, theft, vehicular homicide, addiction, abortion, marriage infidelity, and sexual sin wrack people with guilt. Deadly guilt. Guilt is deadly to your soul on earth, and the guilt of unforgiven sin can take you away from God in the afterlife. Unforgiven sin can keep you from an afterlife with God and have you cast into the torments of a real hell – after tasting it while living.

In Christianity it has been debated – "Are all sins the same?"
Some sins don't hurt as many people, but all sins do have one thing in common: all sin is evil. They are horrible and repugnant to a holy God. They grieved the heart of God so much that He bankrupted the riches of heaven to buy righteousness for your filthy sin-scarred soul. He traded the riches of Christ, His only

son, to pay for your righteousness before God. This agreement happens when you turn from sin and towards God for forgiveness.

This is the gospel. Jesus Christ, who came from heaven, died in your place for punishment of your sin before a holy God. We can now turn to him to be considered righteous before God our Father and live in holiness and receive eternal life.

When we truthfully inspect ourselves and the state of our soul, we might rank our sins from what we view as minor to the worst sins ever committed, perhaps by yourself or others. Every evening, you can view gross sins on the news that are so ghastly they make us recoil when we watch them.

In one way, all sin is the same. It took the shedding of Christ's blood on the cross to receive forgiveness from God that leads to the erasure of sin and your salvation.

Humanity was plunged into the depths of sin, since the beginning of time with our ancestors, Adam and Eve. I want you to know there is a cure for those sins. How do we know this? Jesus told us.

"But you don't know what I have done." That lament has been said by many. That evil logic has kept the healing of the soul from happening for scores of people. Your Creator knows all about you. Rest assured, you are not more bad than Jesus Christ is good!

Look at this example from the Bible that should encourage you. In your sin, you have not gone too far for salvation and healing.

Do you think you have? Then answer these two questions.

Have you ever betrayed God in the flesh in person? Have you ever betrayed Him at His greatest need for your love while He walked this world and carried His cross? Were you ever His friend when He was on earth? Of course not. Yet through Jesus Christ's relationship with Peter, you see that even your sins can be forgiven and your shame can be erased.

Chapter 2

Shame Eraser

Jesus Christ is both like you and not like you at all. Jesus Christ had what Christians have through history called a "dual nature". He was and is fully man and also fully God. In the book of Luke, Jesus knew His earthly ministry as a living man would soon be over. The next day Christ Jesus our Lord knew he would be abandoned, beaten, stripped naked, and mocked while tortured to death on the cross of punishment for law-breakers (us). He would pay to God our sin payment so that unrighteous humanity could put on the righteousness of Christ and enter into eternal life now and one day heaven. Christ Jesus' moment of truth, his personal D-Day, and final assault on evil was now taking place. On the night when He instituted the Lord's Supper or Eucharist ("great thanksgiving") He was seeking fellowship and worship with His close friends.

LUKE 22 --- Jesus institutes the Lord's Supper:

14 When the hour had come, He sat down, and the twelve apostles with Him.

AUTHOR'S NOTE: THE NIGHT BEFORE HIS DEATH AND BATTLE FOR YOUR ETERNAL SOUL, JESUS CHRIST WAS WITH HIS LIEUTENANTS ON HIS WAR AGAINST THE EVIL ONE AND THE DEADLY PLAGUE OF SIN ON HIS CREATION. HOW DO I SEE HIM PRESIDING OVER THIS MEETING? WE ARE NOT

SEEING HERE THE SWEET
JESUS THAT THE OLD HYMN
DESCRIBES AS "GENTLE JESUS,
MEEK AND MILD." THAT
IMAGE OF JESUS CHRIST WAS
NOT PRESENT. WHO PRESIDED
WAS THE JESUS CHRIST, THE
SAVIOR-MESSIAH. THIS IS HOW
THE BIBLE DESCRIBES THE
SECOND PERSON OF THE
GODHEAD OR WHAT
CHRISTIANS CALL THE
TRINITY.

Isaiah 42:13

*13 The Lord shall go forth like a
mighty man;
He shall stir up His zeal like a man
of war.
He shall cry out, yes, shout aloud;
He shall prevail against His
enemies.*

He was playing for keeps or actually fighting for keeps over you. I see THE KING OF GLORY like a boss, a warhorse, sin-hating, humanity loving Savior. His painful mission paid by His own personal cost was about to be completed.

Now we return to Jesus in Luke 22:

15 Then He said to them, "With fervent desire I have desired to eat this Passover with you before I suffer;

16 for I say to you, I will no longer eat of it until it is fulfilled in the kingdom of God."

AUTHORS NOTE: CHRIST HATES SIN AND LOVES WHO HE DIED FOR (YOU) - FERVENTLY.

17 Then He took the cup, and gave thanks, and said, "Take this and divide it among yourselves;

18 for I say to you, I will not drink of the fruit of the vine until the kingdom of God comes."

AUTHOR'S NOTE: CHRIST WILL CELEBRATE WITH THE FRUIT OF THE VINE IN HEAVEN AFTER HIS CRUSHING VICTORY OVER THE POWER OF SATAN. NOW HE WILL SHARE THE FRUIT OF THE VINE WITH HIS FRIENDS AS HE GETS READY FOR THE PHYSICAL, MENTAL, AND SPIRITUAL BATTLE FOR YOUR SOUL THE NEXT DAY.

19 And He took bread, gave thanks and broke it, and gave it to them, saying, "This is My body which is given for you; do this in remembrance of Me."

20 Likewise He also took the cup after supper, saying, "This cup is the new covenant in My blood, which is shed for you.

AUTHOR'S NOTE: THERE IS NOTHING AS INTIMATE AS YOUR RELATIONSHIP WITH CHRIST. HIS WORD SAYS HE IS IN US AND WE ARE IN HIM WHEN WE FELLOWSHIP WITH HIM IN COMMUNION WHICH WE ALSO CALL "THE LORD'S SUPPER."

21 But behold, the hand of My betrayer is with Me on the table.

22 And truly the Son of Man goes as it has been determined, but woe to that man by whom He is betrayed!"

AUTHOR'S NOTE: JUDAS HAD THE ULTIMATE SHAME AND BECAME CURSED. WHY? HE COULD NOT OR WOULD NOT RECEIVE THE LOVE AND FORGIVENESS THAT JESUS CHRIST WAS GOING TO EARN FOR US ON THE CROSS. JUDAS TOOK THE SILVER COINS TO BETRAY HIS TEACHER AND FRIEND, JESUS. JUDAS COULD NOT PURCHASE A CLEAN HEART. WITH HIS BLOOD MONEY, JUDAS RECEIVED THE SPIRIT OF SUICIDE AND THE EVIL ONE. JUDAS TURNED FROM LIFE TO DEATH.

23 Then they began to question among themselves, which of them it was who would do this thing.

CHAPTER 3

GRACE = Christ Died For The Undeserving, US!

AUTHOR'S NOTE: THERE WERE 12 APOSTLES. ONE (JUDAS)WOULD BETRAY JESUS CHRIST THAT NIGHT. THEY ALL WOULD SOON SCATTER AFTER JESUS WAS ARRESTED. THE APOSTLES' DUTY WAS TO SUPPORT THEIR RABBI/TEACHER AND FRIEND AS HE WAS POURING OUT HIS HEART AND BARING HIS SOUL TO THEM. THESE MEN HAD SEEN JESUS RAISE THE DEAD, WALK ON WATER, GIVE SIGHT TO THE BLIND, CAST OUT DEMONS, FEED THOUSANDS OUT OF LITTLE MORE THAN A FEW LOAVES OF BREAD AND A

COUPLE OF FISH. JESUS
CHRIST, THE GREATEST
TEACHER IN HISTORY IS
SPENDING HIS REMAINING
HOURS POURING INTO HIS
LEADERS. THERE IS ONE
PROBLEM HERE. THE 12 MEN
DID NOT "GET IT".
WHAT DO THE DISCIPLES GET
FROM THIS IMPASSIONED
LESSON AND CEREMONY OF
SELFLESSNESS AND
DEVOTION? THEY ALL BEGAN
THINKING AND ASKING "WHAT
IS IN IT FOR ME?" THE
DISCIPLES' GRADE OF
UNDERSTANDING THE GUILT
AND SHAME ERASING MISSION
OF JESUS WAS IN. THE GRADE?
FAILURE WITH A BIG 'F'.

Luke 22 The Disciples Argue About Their Greatness"

24 Now there was also a dispute among them, as to which of them should be considered the greatest.

25 And He said to them, "The kings of the Gentiles exercise lordship over them, and those who exercise authority over them are called 'benefactors'.

26 But not so among you; on the contrary, he who is greatest among you, let him be as the younger, and he who governs as he who serves.

27 For who is greater, he who sits at the table, or he who serves? Is it not he who sits at the table? Yet I am among you as the One who serves.

28 But you are those who have continued with Me in My trials.

29 And I bestow upon you a kingdom, just as My Father bestowed one upon Me,

30 that you may eat and drink at My table in My kingdom, and sit on thrones judging the twelve tribes of Israel."

Jesus Predicts Peter's Denial:

AUTHOR'S NOTE: THE GRACE OF GOD AND THE BLOOD OF CHRIST PAID FOR SINS PAST, PRESENT, AND FUTURE. THE MIGHTY APOSTLE PETER WAS GETTING READY TO SIN AS BADLY AS ANYONE HAS IN HISTORY. OUR GRACIOUS LORD IS READY FOR PETER'S FORGIVNESS & RESTORATION –

EVEN BEFORE HE SINS IN THE
FACE OF JESUS CHRIST. CHRIST
WAS PREPARING TO CARRY
THAT CROSS FOR THE SIN
PETER WOULD COMMIT – AND
YOUR FUTURE SIN!

*31 And the Lord said, "Simon,
Simon! Indeed, Satan has asked for
you, that he may sift you as wheat.*

*32 But I have prayed for you, that
your faith should not fail; and when
you have returned to Me, strengthen
your brethren."*

AUTHOR'S NOTE: JESUS DIED
EVEN FOR FUTURE SHAME –
WE CAN NOT SAY "YOU DON'T
KNOW WHAT IT'S LIKE." HE
WORE OUR SIN ON THE CROSS
AND PAID FOR OUR PENALTY
IN FULL.

*33 But he said to
Him, "Lord, I am ready to go with
You, both to prison and to death."*

*34 Then He said, "I tell you, Peter,
the rooster shall not crow this day
before you will deny three times that
you know Me."*

CHAPTER 4

When Your Actions Do Not Match Your Faith

In John 18 we will look at Jesus Christ's betrayal and arrest in Gethsemane:

JOHN 18

1When Jesus had spoken these words, He went out with His disciples over the Brook Kidron, where there was a garden, which He and His disciples entered.

2 And Judas, who betrayed Him, also knew the place; for Jesus often met there with His disciples.

3 Then Judas, having received a detachment of troops, and officers from the chief priests and Pharisees, came there with lanterns, torches, and weapons.

4 Jesus therefore, knowing all things that would come upon Him, went forward and said to them, "Whom are you seeking?"

5 They answered Him, "Jesus of Nazareth." Jesus said to them, "I am He." And Judas, who betrayed Him, also stood with them.

6 Now when He said to them, "I am He," they drew back and fell to the ground.

AUTHOR'S NOTE: "I AM" WAS HOW GOD DESCRIBED HIMSELF TO MOSES AND THE ANCIENT HEBREWS. WHEN GOD IN THE FLESH, JESUS CHRIST, SAID ONE OF HIS NAMES, "I AM",

THIS MADE "a detachment of troops, and officers from the chief priests and Pharisees" FALL TO THE GROUND.

7 Then He asked them again, "Whom are you seeking?" And they said, "Jesus of Nazareth."

8 Jesus answered, "I have told you that I am He. Therefore, if you seek Me, let these go their way,"

9 that the saying might be fulfilled which He spoke, "Of those whom You gave Me I have lost none."

10 Then Simon Peter, having a sword, drew it and struck the high priest's servant, and cut off his right ear. The servant's name was Malchus.

11 So Jesus said to Peter, "Put your sword into the sheath. Shall I not drink the cup which My Father has given Me?"

AUTHOR'S NOTE: PETER WAS BOLD AND EVEN DEFENDED CHRIST WITH A SWORD. HE HAD FAITH IN HIS FAITH – BUT NOT TRUE FAITH IN CHRIST.

The Savior had been taken away. After being separated from Christ, Peter did what he vowed to Jesus he would never do. He did the worst thing possible – Peter denied Christ!

CHAPTER 5

The Results Of Sin = Shame

Peter, the formerly brave solider for Christ, is now reduced to a weeping coward by the shame of his great sin.

LUKE 22

54 Having arrested Him, they led Him and brought Him into the high priest's house. But Peter followed at a distance.

55 Now when they had kindled a fire in the midst of the courtyard and sat down together, Peter sat among them.

56 And a certain servant girl, seeing him as he sat by the fire, looked intently at him and said, "This man was also with Him."

57 But he denied Him, saying, "Woman, I do not know Him."

58 And after a little while another saw him and said, "You also are of them." But Peter said, "Man, I am not!"

59 Then after about an hour had passed, another confidently affirmed, saying, "Surely this fellow also was with Him, for he is a Galilean."

60 But Peter said, "Man, I do not know what you are saying!" Immediately, while he was still speaking, the rooster crowed.

61 And the Lord turned and looked at Peter. Then Peter remembered the word of the Lord, how He had said to him, "Before the rooster crows, you will deny Me three times."

62 So Peter went out and wept bitterly.

AUTHOR'S NOTE: PETER MUST HAVE EXPERIENCED THE BIGGEST HEART AND SOUL ACHE ANY HUMAN HAS EVER ENDURED. ON PETER'S THIRD DENIAL, THE BLOODY, BEATEN, AND BETRAYED SAVIOR LOCKED EYES WITH PETER AS PETER COMPLETED HIS BETRAYAL - "the Lord turned and looked at Peter."

AUTHOR'S NOTE: PETER HAD FLED. IF HE DID NOT VIEW THE BEATINGS AND MOCKING OF CHRIST JESUS, HE HAD TO HAVE HEARD ABOUT IT. PETER DENIED AND ABANDONED THE ONE HE LOVED MOST.

Jesus Mocked and Beaten:

63 Now the men who held Jesus mocked Him and beat Him.

64 And having blindfolded Him, they struck Him on the face and asked Him,[saying, "Prophesy! Who is the one who struck You?"

65 And many other things they blasphemously spoke against Him.

Jesus Faces the Sanhedrin:

66 As soon as it was day, the elders of the people, both chief priests and scribes, came together and led Him into their council, saying,

67 "If You are the Christ, tell us." But He said to them, "If I tell you, you will by no means believe.

68 And if I also ask you, you will by no means answer Me or let Me go.

69 Hereafter the Son of Man will sit on the right hand of the power of God."

70 Then they all said, "Are You then the Son of God?"
So He said to them, "You rightly say that I am."

71 And they said, "What further testimony do we need? For we have heard it ourselves from His own mouth."

CHAPTER 6

Shame and Guilt of Sin

LUKE 22

61 And the Lord turned and looked at Peter. Then Peter remembered the word of the Lord, how He had said to him, "Before the rooster crows, you will deny Me three times."

62 So Peter went out and wept bitterly.

Peter previously thought he was the head of the parade of the winning team. He served his master and teacher, Jesus of Nazareth, who was mighty in word and deed. Earlier Jesus was preaching great lessons, healing the sick, giving sight to the blind, walking on water and raising the dead. Peter could not lose. We can get lost in the blessings of God and we lose focus of what GRACE truly is. Like it has been taught for years, grace is God's unmerited favor. This is why we worship. Our Savior did what we could not do for ourselves in our sinful state. Christ Jesus saved us sinners from the penalty of death, the curse of sin, and reunited us with the Father.

Ephesians 2:8-10

8 For by grace you have been saved through faith, and that not of yourselves; it is the gift of God,

9 not of works, lest anyone should boast.

10 For we are His workmanship, created in Christ Jesus for good works, which God prepared

beforehand that we should walk in them.

Unfortunately the arrogance Peter developed before his great fall could have been stopped by heeding the teachings of Christ and Scripture. In his youth, surly Peter had read:

Genesis 4:7

6 So the Lord said to Cain, "Why are you angry? And why has your countenance fallen?

7 If you do well, will you not be accepted? And if you do not do well, sin lies at the door. And its desire is for you, but you should rule over it."

After his impulsive betrayal of Jesus, Peter

remembered the warning of Christ in Luke 22:

31 And the Lord said, "Simon, Simon! Indeed, Satan has asked for you, that he may sift you as wheat.

Peter probably remembered the warning, but he forgot the medicine – the healing balm of Christ.

32 But I have prayed for you, that your faith should not fail; and when you have returned to Me, strengthen your brethren."

So how did Peter feel? He committed the worst sin. He had fallen from his lofty position as a leader of the disciples. This type of tremendous stress and guilt leads people to suicide. There is a famous study in Sociology about suicide by Emile Durkheim. The concept of "Anomie" is mentioned. This study describes anomie as an absence of value in society. A person feels like a rat in the corner that cannot strike back. Nobody understands them. They have lost the values and sense of self-worth. The evil one wins a victory over a life that Christ came to redeem.

Hopeless – unforgivable – embarrassment of your ethical character – the pain of hurting the one you love – these are all self-inflicted and demonically influenced emotions. You feel totally alone. A friend cannot help you. The evil one will fight to keep you from your only help and means. Defeat is separation from Christ, but victory is at hand by turning to Jesus Christ.

The covenant promise was sealed with the blood of Jesus Christ on the

cross. God's shame erasing power is
proven in the power of Jesus Christ
in the Resurrection.

CHAPTER 7

The Cost Of Sin And The Brutal Death Of Christ

AUTHOR'S NOTE: JESUS RECEIVED MOCKING & HUMILIATION IN YOUR PLACE.

John 19

1 So then Pilate took Jesus and scourged Him.

2 And the soldiers twisted a crown of thorns and put it on His head, and they put on Him a purple robe.

3 Then they said, "Hail, King of the Jews!" And they struck Him with their hands.

4 Pilate then went out again, and said to them, "Behold, I am bringing Him out to you, that you may know that I find no fault in Him."

AUTHOR'S NOTE: JESUS WAS JUDGED UNFAIRLY BY BAD PEOPLE - IN YOUR PLACE.

5 Then Jesus came out, wearing the crown of thorns and the purple robe. And Pilate said to them, "Behold the Man!"

6 Therefore, when the chief priests and officers saw Him, they cried out, saying, "Crucify Him, crucify Him!"
Pilate said to them, "You take Him and crucify Him, for I find no fault in Him."

7 The Jews answered him, "We have a law, and according to our law He ought to die, because He made Himself the Son of God."

8 Therefore, when Pilate heard that saying, he was the more afraid,

9 and went again into the Praetorium, and said to Jesus, "Where are You from?" But Jesus gave him no answer.

10 Then Pilate said to Him, "Are You not speaking to me? Do You not know that I have power to crucify You, and power to release You?"

11 Jesus answered, "You could have no power at all against Me unless it had been given you from above. Therefore the one who delivered Me to you has the greater sin."

12 From then on Pilate sought to release Him, but the Jews cried out, saying, "If you let this Man go, you are not Caesar's friend. Whoever makes himself a king speaks against Caesar."

13 When Pilate therefore heard that saying, he brought Jesus out and sat down in the judgment seat in a place that is called The Pavement, but in Hebrew, Gabbatha.

14 Now it was the Preparation Day of the Passover, and about the sixth hour. And he said to the Jews, "Behold your King!"

15 But they cried out, "Away with Him, away with Him! Crucify Him!"
Pilate said to them, "Shall I crucify your King?"

The chief priests answered, "We have no king but Caesar!"

16 Then he delivered Him to them to be crucified. Then they took Jesus and led Him away.

AUTHOR'S NOTE: ROMAN SOLIDERS STRIPPED JESUS OF HIS PURPLE ROYAL ROBE. THAT MATCHED CHRIST'S FURTHER MOCKERY OF HIS ROYALTY BY HIS CROWN OF THORNS THE SOILDERS SMASHED ON HIS HEAD. THE SOILDERS LATER GAMBLED FOR HIS TUNIC. JESUS WAS EMBARASSED AND EXPOSED NAKED TO THE WHOLE WORLD – HE DID THIS IN YOUR PLACE.

17 And He, bearing His cross, went out to a place called the Place of a Skull, which is called in Hebrew, Golgotha,

18 where they crucified Him, and two others with Him, one on either side, and Jesus in the center.

19 Now Pilate wrote a title and put it on the cross. And the writing was:
JESUS OF NAZARETH, THE KING OF THE JEWS.

20 Then many of the Jews read this title, for the place where Jesus was crucified was near the city; and it was written in Hebrew, Greek, and Latin.

21 Therefore the chief priests of the Jews said to Pilate, "Do not write, 'The King of the Jews,' but, 'He said, "I am the King of the Jews." '"

22 Pilate answered, "What I have written, I have written."

AUTHOR'S NOTE: JESUS WAS HUMILIATED IN FRONT OF ALL OF SOCIETY. EVERYONE KNEW AND SAW HIS SHAME. HE DID THIS IN YOUR PLACE.

23 Then the soldiers, when they had crucified Jesus, took His garments and made four parts, to each soldier a part, and also the tunic. Now the tunic was without seam, woven from the top in one piece.

24 They said therefore among themselves, "Let us not tear it, but cast lots for it, whose it shall be," that the Scripture might be fulfilled which says:
"They divided My garments among them,
And for My clothing they cast lots."
Therefore the soldiers did these things.

Behold Your Mother:

25 Now there stood by the cross of Jesus His mother, and His mother's sister, Mary the wife of Clopas, and Mary Magdalene.

26 When Jesus therefore saw His mother, and the disciple whom He loved standing by, He said to His mother, "Woman, behold your son!"

27 Then He said to the disciple, "Behold your mother!" And from that hour that disciple took her to his own home.

AUTHOR'S NOTE: JESUS DIED A REAL AND EXCRUCIATING DEATH FOR CRIMES AND SINS – IN YOUR PLACE.

28 After this, Jesus, knowing that all things were now accomplished, that the Scripture might be fulfilled, said, "I thirst!"

29 Now a vessel full of sour wine was sitting there; and they filled a sponge with sour wine, put it on hyssop, and put it to His mouth.

30 So when Jesus had received the sour wine, He said, "It is finished!" And bowing His head, He gave up His spirit.

AUTHOR'S NOTE: JESUS WAS INNOCENT OF ANY SIN. HUMANS ARE SINNERS. JESUS TASTED DEATH DUE TO THE CURSE OF YOUR SIN – IN YOUR PLACE.

31 Therefore, because it was the Preparation Day, that the bodies should not remain on the cross on the Sabbath (for that Sabbath was a high day), the Jews asked Pilate that their legs might be broken, and that they might be taken away.

32 Then the soldiers came and broke the legs of the first and of the other who was crucified with Him.

33 But when they came to Jesus and saw that He was already dead, they did not break His legs.

34 But one of the soldiers pierced His side with a spear, and immediately blood and water came out.

35 And he who has seen has testified, and his testimony is true; and he knows that he is telling the truth, so that you may believe.

36 For these things were done that the Scripture should be fulfilled, "Not one of His bones shall be broken."

37 And again another Scripture says, "They shall look on Him whom they pierced."

Chapter 8

Your Sin

Believer's sin were erased on the cross. Their sins were not just dismissed. Sin was disgusting and something to be hidden and covered with shame. Sin, it drove a wedge between God and man's relationship. Sin too often is related to a Greek word that talks about how we passively "missed the mark." Humanity did not just miss the mark. We waved our fist before God and said we will maintain our lusts, violate holy laws, and maintain that our desires are more important than anything or anyone.

Sin is serious and it dooms us. We sin by choice.

1 John 3:4

4 Whoever commits sin also commits lawlessness, and sin is lawlessness.
God hates sin and cannot abide with it.

Deuteronomy 9:7

7 Remember! Do not forget how you provoked the Lord your God to wrath in the wilderness. From the day that you departed from the land of Egypt until you came to this place, you have been rebellious against the Lord.

Sin kills us:

Joshua 1:18

18 Whoever rebels against your command and does not heed your words, in all that you command him, shall be put to death. Only be strong and of good courage.

SIN KILLS US!

Romans 5:12

12 Therefore, just as through one man sin entered the world, and death through sin, and thus death spread to all men, because all sinned

Romans 6:23

23 For the wages of sin is death, but the gift of God is eternal life in Christ Jesus our Lord.

God loves you, His creation, more than he hates sin. Your sin was dealt with by the greatest act of love and the greatest price possible. The vault

of treasures in heaven was broken
and given to purchase your innocence
and pay your sin debt to satisfy the
wrath of God.

Ephesians 1:7

*7 In Him we have redemption
through His blood, the forgiveness
of sins, according to the riches of
His grace*

You know your sin. It dogs you.
Perhaps no one else knows, or you
may feel like everyone knows. It
might seem unremarkable, or your
sin might have landed you in jail.

Some of the harm sin has done to you:

#1. Sin separated you from God.

#2. Sin has broken relationships with family and friends.

#3. Sin has hurt others.

#4. Sin has left you with guilt and shame.

#5. Sin is what the road to hell is really paved with.

You know your sin.
You are guilty.
You know there is a Savior who did EVERYTHING to pardon your sin and restore you.

What will you do?

CHAPTER 9

Your Forgiveness

In the gospel book of Mark, a young man, who we presume to be an angel, is seen clothed in a long white robe sitting on the right side of the empty tomb on Sunday the day after the Jewish Sabbath has ended.(The resurrection day we call Easter.) The tomb is empty. Jesus Christ, the victor over death, hell, and the grave, the one who purchased our salvation with His death, is not in the tomb. It is empty! A messenger gives some of the followers of Jesus a message.

Mark 16

4 But when they looked up, they saw that the stone had been rolled away—for it was very large.

5 And entering the tomb, they saw a young man clothed in a long white robe sitting on the right side; and they were alarmed.

6 But he said to them, "Do not be alarmed. You seek Jesus of Nazareth, who was crucified. He is risen! He is not here. See the place where they laid Him.

7 But go, tell His disciples—and Peter—that He is going before you into Galilee; there you will see Him, as He said to you."

The book of John gives us this gorgeous and beautiful story of the perfect restoration that only Jesus Christ can give to Peter.

John 21

Breakfast by the Sea:

1 After these things Jesus showed Himself again to the disciples at the Sea of Tiberias, and in this way He showed Himself:

2 Simon Peter, Thomas called the Twin, Nathanael of Cana in Galilee, the sons of Zebedee, and two others of His disciples were together.

3 Simon Peter said to them, "I am going fishing."
They said to him, "We are going with you also." They went out and immediately got into the boat, and that night they caught nothing.

4 But when the morning had now come, Jesus stood on the shore; yet the disciples did not know that it was Jesus.

5 Then Jesus said to them, "Children, have you any food?"
They answered Him, "No."

6 And He said to them, "Cast the net on the right side of the boat, and you will find some." So, they cast, and now they were not able to draw it in because of the multitude of fish.

7 Therefore that disciple whom Jesus loved said to Peter, "It is the Lord!" Now when Simon Peter heard that it was the Lord, he put on his outer garment (for he had removed it), and plunged into the sea.

8 But the other disciples came in the little boat (for they were not far from land, but about two hundred cubits), dragging the net with fish.

9 Then, as soon as they had come to land, they saw a fire of coals there, and fish laid on it, and bread.

10 Jesus said to them, "Bring some of the fish which you have just caught."

11 Simon Peter went up and dragged the net to land, full of large fish, one hundred and fifty-three; and although there were so many, the net was not broken.

12 Jesus said to them, "Come and eat breakfast." Yet none of the disciples dared ask Him, "Who are You?"—knowing that it was the Lord.

13 Jesus then came and took the bread and gave it to them, and likewise the fish.

14 This is now the third time Jesus showed Himself to His disciples after He was raised from the dead.

Author's Note: THERE HAD TO BE A COMING TOGETHER BETWEEN THE LORD AND PETER BEFORE JESUS RESTORES PETER. HAVE YOU MET WITH THE LORD?

15 So when they had eaten breakfast, Jesus said to Simon Peter, "Simon, son of Jonah, do you love Me more than these?"
He said to Him, "Yes, Lord; You know that I love You."
He said to him, "Feed My lambs."

16 He said to him again a second time, "Simon, son of Jonah, do you love Me?"
He said to Him, "Yes, Lord; You know that I love You."
He said to him, "Tend My sheep."

17 He said to him the third time, "Simon, son of Jonah, do you love Me?" Peter was grieved because He said to him the third time, "Do you love Me?"

AUTHOR'S NOTE: THIS RESTORATION IS A MATTER OF THE HEART AND THE SOUL. IT GRIEVED PETER TO LOOK AT HIS SINFUL ACTIONS. THERE IS PAIN IN HEALING, BUT THERE IS MORE PAIN IN SIN, SICKNESS, AND DEATH. THIS WAS WHERE IT HAPPENED. THREE TIMES PETER DENIED JESUS. THREE TIMES THE

SAVIOR RESTORED PETER. CAN YOU DO THE SAME?

17 And he said to Him, "Lord, You know all things; You know that I love You."
Jesus said to him, "Feed My sheep.

18 Most assuredly, I say to you, when you were younger, you girded yourself and walked where you wished; but when you are old, you will stretch out your hands, and another will gird you and carry you where you do not wish."

19 This He spoke, signifying by what death he would glorify God. And when He had spoken this, He said to him, "Follow Me."

WILL YOU BE RESTORED AND HAVE YOUR SHAME ERASED BY FOLLOWING JESUS?

CHAPTER 10

Guilt of Cancelled Sin

To remember his one-year anniversary of his shame being erased, in 1734 Charles Wesley wrote the hymn
'O For A Thousand Tongues To Sing',
This following verse is good news to the downcast Christian living in guilt:

"He breaks the power of canceled sin,
He sets the prisoner free;
His blood can make the foulest clean,
His blood availed for me."

Your sin has been canceled in the eyes of God and His eternal record. This hymn speaks to Christians about being able to let go of past forgiven sins and to live a guiltless life.

Are past sins still haunting you? Do you think you should live like you are guiltless? Do you deserve it? Christ's blood says "yes"; you deserve it because you received justification by the blood of Jesus. How?
He has taken, carried, and worn our sin on the cross. Christ took our punishment so that we can be made right with God.
We who turned away from sin and towards Christ have been justified and will be judged by not our sinful past but by the spotless, sinless record of Christ Jesus our Savior.

That deserves repeating. How can this be? Before the throne in heaven, you are declared sinless in the legal sense because your record that was deserving of punishment is now clean. This is called your JUSTIFICATION made possible only by Jesus Christ.

Here is more good news.
You are declared righteous by God, not by your actions. Peter tried to supply his own righteousness by his actions. He was a bold outspoken esteemed leader of the followers of Jesus.

Christ Jesus had to rebuke Peter. Christ told him that Peter's way did not coincide with Christ's path to the cross.

Matthew 16

21 From that time Jesus began to show to His disciples that He must go to Jerusalem, and suffer many things from the elders and chief priests and scribes, and be killed, and be raised the third day.

22 Then Peter took Him aside and began to rebuke Him, saying, "Far be it from You, Lord; this shall not happen to You!"

23 But He turned and said to Peter, "Get behind Me, Satan! You are an offense to Me, for you are not mindful of the things of God, but the things of men."

In heaven today, Peter is glad he was proven gloriously wrong. Our shame is erased only because of Jesus.

We are guiltless and we should celebrate.
Why?
Because Jesus the RIGHTEOUS has declared us innocent and worthy.
Let the gloom and guilt be cast away.

This is why we worship and celebrate the King of kings and Lord of lords.

CHAPTER 11

Your Justification
For Receiving Forgiveness

Did you help with a food drive,
collect coats for the homeless, or
raise money to support storm
victims? Those are good things to do.
They are things Christians often do
and even community-minded non-
Christians.

The point is, good deeds can show
what you support.
We are sinful people.
We can never do enough good deeds
to erase our sin, shame, and earn
salvation.

That is why Jesus Christ is our
Savior.
He paid the payment for our sin.
He did what we can never do.

He erased our sin, shame, and guilt.
You can give a clear answer when
you are asked, "Why do you think
you will go to heaven when you die?"

You are JUSTIFIED by Jesus Christ
and his atoning death on the cross.
He paid our sin debt and declares His
people righteous before the Father.
That is justification.

2 Corinthians 5:21

*21 For He made Him who knew no
sin to be sin for us, that we might
become the righteousness of God in
Him.*

2 Corinthians 5:18-19

*18 Now all things are of God, who
has reconciled us to Himself
through Jesus Christ, and has given
us the ministry of reconciliation,*

19 that is, that God was in Christ reconciling the world to Himself, not imputing their trespasses to them, and has committed to us the word of reconciliation.

Jesus paid the price for our salvation.

Matthew 20

28 just as the Son of Man did not come to be served, but to serve, and to give His life a ransom for many.

Jesus Christ is our Savior. Do you need your shame erased?

CHAPTER 12

How To Have Your Shame Erased

To turn from wrong-thinking, to turn from sin to Christ is called repenting. The solution to your shame and guilt will not happen by positive thinking or counseling.

Jesus Christ made it simple.

Mark 1:15

And saying, "The time is fulfilled, and the kingdom of God is at hand. Repent, and believe in the gospel."

Turn from your sins to the One who paid the price for your shame to be erased. The American way of life will tell you that you must earn a reward. In trying to earn forgiveness you will only earn frustration and tears. You will learn you cannot achieve erasure of sin and shame. Good. Now you know the truth. Jesus Christ did what you could not do for yourself. He took your punishment on the cross. The wrath of God and His law are satisfied. The hard part is, at the same time, the easy part. You must confess to receive the benefits of the salvation that you cannot produce. You/we produced sin. Jesus Christ produced salvation.

Honor God. Trust that His Son's blood will pay for sins past, present and future. Salvation is simple; We make it hard. You have heard the Good News or Gospel. Jesus Christ, God in the flesh, died in your place to pay for your sins to satisfy God's wrath against sin and sinners. When you believe you are forgiven, you have peace with God and inherit eternal life. Trust you are justified before God now because you have the assurance of the blood of Jesus. Do not dishonor God and believe the goodness and righteousness of His Son's blood are not enough to cover your sin and shame.

How do you respond to knowing you can have your sin and shame erased?

(A) Admit you are a sinner.

(B) Believe Jesus Christ is Lord (God in the flesh) and his blood paid your sin debt. Ask for His forgiveness for sins you willingly and unintentionally committed.

(C) Confess Christ publicly

Romans 10:9-10

"...that if you confess with your mouth the Lord Jesus and believe in your heart that God has raised Him from the dead, you will be saved. For with the heart one believes unto righteousness, and with the mouth confession is made unto salvation."

Have your shame and sin erased.

Receive the good news!